Macroeconomics Explained in 10 Minutes

Roggie Clark

Get Out of Credit Card Debt With This Book

Are you tired of living paycheck to paycheck? Drowning in interest rates and minimum payments that never seem to shrink your balance? *Understanding & Overcoming Credit Card Debt* is your roadmap to financial freedom.

https://www.amazon.com/dp/B0F3WCVWG8

Avoid Wasting Money On Crypto With This Book

Whether you're curious, cautious, or ready to invest, this book breaks down complex topics into plain language and cuts through the noise, buzzwords, and get-rich-quick schemes.

https://www.amazon.com/Think-Before-You-Crypto-Understanding-ebook/dp/B0F3YQ1L2Q

Learn How To Invest in Gold Bars With This Book

Whether you're new to investing or seeking to diversify your portfolio, this beginner-friendly guide will give you the knowledge and confidence to invest in gold, and other precious metals.

https://www.amazon.com/Ultimate-Investing-Buying-Guide-Beginners-ebook/dp/B0F1KWWDXG

Learn How To Invest in Silver With This Book

Whether you're approaching retirement or already enjoying it, protecting and growing your wealth is critical. The Ultimate Silver Investing & Buying Guide For Beginners is your clear, no-nonsense guide to incorporating silver into your wealth-building strategy.

https://www.amazon.com/Ultimate-Silver-Investing-Buying-Beginners-ebook

Copyright

Title: Macroeconomics Explained in 10 Minutes
Author: Roggie Clark

Disclaimer

The views and opinions expressed in this book are those of the author and do not necessarily reflect the official policy or position of any individual, company, or organization cited or referenced in the text. The author is not affiliated with any of the individuals, companies, or organizations mentioned in the text, nor does the author receive any form of compensation for citing or referencing them.

The professional information in this text is distributed on an "as is" basis, without warranty. While every precaution has been taken in the preparation of the text, neither the author nor the publisher shall have any liability to any person or entity with respect to any loss or damage caused or alleged to be caused directly or indirectly by the instructions contained in this text or by the computer software and hardware products described in it.

The author nor the publisher does not guarantee any specific results or outcomes, and the information provided in this text should not be construed as professional advice. Readers should always consult with a qualified professional before making any significant changes to their website or business.

By reading this text, you agree that the author nor the publisher is responsible for any direct, indirect, incidental, or consequential damages that may arise from the use of the information provided. You assume full responsibility for any actions taken based on the information presented in this text.

Table of Contents

Chapter 1: The Big Idea: What Macroeconomics Really Is

Most people hear words like inflation, recession, or interest rates and feel like the economy is something distant or complicated. It sounds like something controlled by governments, discussed on the news, and understood only by experts.

But in reality, macroeconomics is not far away from you at all. It shows up in your everyday life, in the prices you pay, the job market, and even how far your money goes. This chapter breaks everything down so you can quickly understand what macroeconomics actually is and why it matters.

What Macroeconomics Means (In Plain English)

Macroeconomics is the study of the overall economy. Instead of focusing on individual decisions like microeconomics, it looks at the big picture.

It focuses on things like:

- The total growth of the economy
- The overall level of prices
- Employment and job opportunities
- National and global economic trends

In simple terms, macroeconomics is about how the economy is performing as a whole, not just what one person or one business is doing.

The Difference Between Micro and Macro (Quickly Explained)

It helps to quickly separate microeconomics from macroeconomics.

- Microeconomics focuses on individual choices, like what you buy or how a business sets prices
- Macroeconomics focuses on the bigger system, like inflation, unemployment, and economic growth

You can think of it like this:

- Micro looks at the pieces
- Macro looks at the entire system

Both are connected, but macroeconomics helps you understand the environment those individual decisions are happening in.

Why the Economy Impacts Your Everyday Life

Even if you never think about economics, it is constantly affecting you.

You experience macroeconomics through:

- The cost of groceries and everyday goods
- Changes in rent, housing prices, and interest rates
- Job availability and wage growth
- The overall cost of living

For example, if inflation rises, your money buys less. If the economy slows down, job opportunities may become more limited. These are not abstract ideas, they are real effects that shape everyday decisions.

The Big Focus: Growth, Stability, and Change

At a high level, macroeconomics is focused on three main ideas:

- Growth, how the economy expands over time
- Stability, how steady or unstable the economy is
- Change, how the economy reacts to shocks, trends, and policies

An economy that is growing steadily with low inflation and stable employment is generally considered healthy. But economies do not stay in one state forever. They move, adjust, and sometimes become unstable.

Understanding these three ideas helps you make sense of what is happening when you hear about economic news or changes in the market.

Last Thoughts

Macroeconomics is not about memorizing complicated theories or trying to predict the future perfectly. It is about understanding the big picture forces that shape your financial reality. When you start to see how growth, inflation, and economic conditions affect your daily life, the subject becomes much more practical and much easier to follow. As you move forward, keep this in mind: macroeconomics is the backdrop for every financial decision you make, whether you realize it or not.

Chapter 2: How the Economy Grows (and Slows Down)

The economy is not static. It does not stay the same year after year. Sometimes it grows, sometimes it slows down, and sometimes it contracts. These changes affect everything from job opportunities to business profits to how confident people feel about spending money. Understanding how and why the economy grows or slows down gives you a clearer picture of what is happening around you.

What Economic Growth Actually Means

Economic growth simply means that the economy is producing more over time. More goods, more services, and more overall activity.

When the economy grows:

- Businesses are producing more
- People are earning more income
- Spending tends to increase

Growth is often measured by how much total output increases, but you do not need to focus on the technical side. The key idea is simple, a growing economy usually means more opportunities and more activity.

What Causes an Economy to Expand

Economic growth does not happen randomly. It is driven by a few key factors working together.

Growth is typically fueled by:

- Increased consumer spending
- Business investment in new products, technology, or expansion
- Government spending on infrastructure and programs
- Innovation that improves efficiency and productivity

For example, if businesses invest in better technology, they can produce more with the same resources. This can lead to higher output and economic expansion.

What Causes an Economy to Slow Down

Just as the economy can grow, it can also slow down. This usually happens when activity starts to decrease.

Common reasons for a slowdown include:

- Reduced consumer spending
- Businesses cutting back on investment
- Rising costs that limit production or consumption
- Uncertainty about the future

When people and businesses become more cautious, they tend to spend less. This reduction in spending can ripple through the economy, slowing things down.

Why Growth Is Not Always Smooth

Economic growth does not happen in a straight line. It moves in waves.

You might see:

- Periods of strong growth
- Periods of slower growth
- Occasional downturns

These fluctuations happen because the factors that drive the economy are always changing. Consumer confidence shifts, businesses adjust their strategies, and external events can impact the system.

This is why the economy feels unpredictable at times, but when you zoom out, you can see patterns in how it expands and slows over time.

Last Thoughts

Economic growth is one of the central ideas in macroeconomics, but it is not constant or guaranteed. It depends on the behavior of consumers, businesses, and broader conditions. When you understand what drives growth and what causes slowdowns, you begin to see the bigger forces shaping the economy. As you move forward, keep this in mind: the economy is always moving, and those movements influence opportunities, risks, and decisions in real life.

Chapter 3: Inflation: Why Prices Rise Over Time

At some point, everyone notices that things cost more than they used to. Groceries, rent, gas, and everyday expenses seem to increase over time. This is not random, and it is not just businesses raising prices for no reason. This is inflation. Understanding inflation helps you see why your money does not go as far as it once did and why prices tend to rise over time.

What Inflation Really Is

Inflation is the general increase in prices across the economy over time. It does not mean that just one product becomes more expensive, it means that many prices are rising together.

In simple terms:

- Prices go up
- The value of money goes down

If something that used to cost ten dollars now costs twelve, your money is not stretching as far as it did before. That is inflation in action.

Why Your Money Buys Less Over Time

As inflation increases, the purchasing power of your money decreases. Purchasing power simply means how much you can buy with a certain amount of money.

When inflation rises:

- Each dollar buys fewer goods and services
- Everyday expenses feel more expensive
- People may need to adjust their spending habits

For example, if your income stays the same but prices rise, you are effectively able to afford less than before. This is why inflation has a direct impact on your daily life.

What Causes Inflation to Increase

Inflation can happen for several reasons, but it usually comes down to an imbalance between demand and supply across the economy.

Some common causes include:

- Increased demand for goods and services across the economy

- Rising costs for businesses, such as materials or labor
- Expansion of the money supply
- Supply disruptions that limit availability

For example, if demand increases rapidly but supply cannot keep up, businesses may raise prices. If it becomes more expensive for businesses to produce goods, those higher costs are often passed on to consumers.

When Inflation Becomes a Problem

A small amount of inflation is normal in a growing economy. But when inflation rises too quickly, it can create problems.

High inflation can lead to:

- Reduced purchasing power
- Uncertainty about future prices
- Difficulty for businesses and consumers to plan

In more extreme cases, rapid inflation can make it difficult for people to keep up with the cost of living, especially if wages do not increase at the same pace.

This is why controlling inflation is a major focus for policymakers and central banks.

Last Thoughts

Inflation is one of the most important concepts in macroeconomics because it directly affects your money. It influences how far your income goes, how businesses set prices, and how the overall economy behaves. When you understand inflation, you start to see why prices change over time and how those changes impact your financial decisions. As you move forward, remember this: inflation is not just about higher prices, it is about the changing value of money itself.

Chapter 4: Recessions, Booms, and Economic Cycles

The economy does not grow at a steady pace forever. It moves through periods of expansion and contraction. Sometimes things are going well, jobs are plentiful, businesses are growing, and people are spending. Other times, things slow down, businesses pull back, and uncertainty increases. These shifts are known as economic cycles, and understanding them helps you make sense of why the economy feels strong at times and weak at others.

What a Recession Actually Is

A recession is a period when economic activity declines. It is not just one thing going wrong, it is a broad slowdown across the economy.

During a recession, you may see:

- Businesses earning less revenue
- Job opportunities becoming more limited
- Consumers spending less money

Recessions can vary in severity. Some are mild and short-lived, while others are deeper and last longer. But the core idea is the same, overall economic activity is decreasing.

What a Boom Looks Like

A boom is the opposite of a recession. It is a period of strong economic growth and high activity.

During a boom, you will often see:

- Increased hiring and job opportunities
- Higher consumer spending
- Business expansion and investment

In these periods, confidence is usually high. People are more willing to spend, and businesses are more willing to take risks and grow.

Why Economies Move in Cycles

The economy moves in cycles because the factors that drive it are always changing.

These cycles are influenced by:

- Consumer confidence and spending habits
- Business investment decisions

- Changes in costs and prices
- External events and uncertainty

For example, when people feel confident about the future, they spend more, which supports growth. When uncertainty increases, people may spend less, which can slow the economy down.

This back and forth creates a cycle of expansion and contraction over time.

What Triggers Economic Downturns

Economic downturns do not happen without reason. They are usually triggered by shifts that disrupt normal activity.

Common triggers include:

- Sharp increases in costs, such as inflation or interest rates
- Sudden drops in consumer or business confidence
- Financial instability or market disruptions
- External shocks that impact production or demand

These triggers can cause businesses and consumers to pull back, which slows economic activity and can lead to a recession.

Last Thoughts

Economic cycles are a natural part of how the economy functions. Periods of growth and slowdown are not unusual, they are expected. When you understand how recessions and booms work, you can better interpret what is happening in the economy and avoid reacting emotionally to short-term changes. As you move forward, remember this: the economy moves in patterns, and recognizing those patterns gives you a clearer perspective on both risk and opportunity.

Chapter 5: Who Controls the Economy (and How)

It can sometimes feel like the economy moves on its own, but there are forces that try to guide it. Governments and central banks play a major role in influencing how the economy grows, slows down, or stabilizes. They cannot control everything, but they can shape the direction of the economy through policies and decisions. Understanding who these players are and how they operate helps you make sense of changes in interest rates, inflation, and overall economic conditions.

The Role of Governments

Governments influence the economy through spending, taxation, and policy decisions. Their goal is usually to support growth, maintain stability, and respond to economic challenges.

Governments can impact the economy by:

- Increasing spending to stimulate economic activity
- Reducing or increasing taxes to influence consumer and business behavior

- Funding projects like infrastructure, education, and public services

For example, during an economic slowdown, a government might increase spending or reduce taxes to encourage more activity and boost demand.

The Role of Central Banks

Central banks are responsible for managing the money supply and helping control inflation. They operate separately from everyday government functions and focus on maintaining economic stability.

Their main goals often include:

- Keeping inflation under control
- Supporting stable economic growth
- Promoting a healthy financial system

They do this by adjusting key tools that influence how money flows through the economy.

Interest Rates Made Simple

One of the most important tools central banks use is interest rates. Interest rates affect how expensive it is to borrow money.

When interest rates are low:

- Borrowing is cheaper
- Consumers and businesses are more likely to spend and invest
- Economic activity tends to increase

When interest rates are high:

- Borrowing becomes more expensive
- Spending and investment may slow down
- Inflation may begin to decrease

This is one of the main ways central banks try to balance growth and inflation.

How Policy Decisions Affect You

Even if you are not paying attention to policy decisions, they are still affecting your daily life.

You may notice these effects through:

- Changes in loan and credit card interest rates

- Shifts in job availability and wages
- Changes in the cost of living
- Fluctuations in housing and investment markets

For example, if interest rates rise, mortgages and loans become more expensive, which can reduce spending. If rates fall, borrowing becomes easier, which can increase economic activity.

Last Thoughts

Governments and central banks do not control every outcome in the economy, but they play a significant role in shaping its direction. Through spending, taxation, and interest rate decisions, they influence how money moves and how the economy responds to challenges. When you understand these roles, you gain a clearer view of why economic conditions change over time. As you move forward, remember this: policy decisions are one of the key forces behind the shifts you see in the economy.

Chapter 6: The Big Picture: How Everything Connects

By now, you have seen each part of the economy on its own. Growth, inflation, economic cycles, and policy decisions can all be understood individually. But in the real world, they are all connected. When one thing changes, it often triggers a chain reaction across the entire system. This is where macroeconomics starts to make the most sense, when you stop seeing separate ideas and start seeing how they work together.

How Inflation, Growth, and Policy Work Together

The economy is shaped by the interaction between three major forces:

- Economic growth
- Inflation
- Policy decisions

These forces are constantly influencing each other.

For example:

- Strong economic growth can increase demand, which may push inflation higher
- Rising inflation may lead central banks to raise interest rates
- Higher interest rates can slow down borrowing and spending, which can reduce growth

This creates a continuous cycle where each part affects the others.

Why One Change Can Affect Everything

A single change in the economy rarely stays isolated. It spreads through the system.

For example:

- A rise in interest rates can reduce spending
- Reduced spending can slow business growth
- Slower business growth can impact hiring

What starts as one decision can influence multiple areas of the economy.

This is why the economy can feel complex, but the underlying idea is simple, everything is connected.

How the Economy Impacts Jobs, Wages, and Costs

Macroeconomics is not just about numbers, it directly affects your everyday life.

You will see its impact in:

- Job availability during periods of growth or recession
- Wage increases or stagnation depending on economic conditions
- Rising or falling costs of living due to inflation

For example, during strong economic growth, businesses may hire more and wages may rise. During a slowdown, hiring may decrease and wage growth may slow.

Thinking About the Economy in Real Life

You do not need to analyze charts to understand the economy. You just need to start paying attention to patterns.

When you hear economic news, ask yourself:

- Is the economy growing or slowing down?

- Is inflation rising or falling?
- What are policymakers doing in response?

These simple questions help you connect the dots and understand what is happening beneath the surface.

Last Thoughts

Macroeconomics becomes much clearer when you see how everything fits together. Growth, inflation, and policy decisions are not separate forces, they are part of the same system. When you begin to recognize how one change can affect multiple areas, you gain a deeper understanding of the economy as a whole. As you move forward, remember this: the economy is a connected system, and understanding those connections is the key to seeing the bigger picture.

Chapter 7: Conclusion: What You Should Take Away

By now, you have seen that macroeconomics is not as complicated as it first appears. It is not about memorizing technical terms or trying to predict every economic move. It is about understanding the big picture, how the economy grows, why prices rise, why downturns happen, and how policy decisions influence everything around you. When you focus on these core ideas, the subject becomes much more practical and much easier to follow.

The Core Ideas to Remember

If you take nothing else from this book, focus on these core ideas:

- The economy moves through periods of growth and slowdown
- Inflation reduces the purchasing power of money over time
- Economic cycles include booms and recessions
- Governments and central banks influence the direction of the economy

These ideas form the foundation of how the economy operates.

How to Understand Economic News and Trends

Economic news can feel overwhelming, but it becomes easier when you know what to look for.

When you hear about the economy, focus on a few key questions:

- Is the economy growing or slowing down?
- Is inflation increasing or decreasing?
- Are interest rates rising or falling?

These questions help you filter out noise and focus on what actually matters.

How to Think About Inflation, Growth, and Risk

Macroeconomics is not just about understanding the present, it is also about thinking ahead.

You can use these ideas to:

- Recognize how inflation affects your money over time
- Understand how economic growth impacts opportunities
- Be more aware of risks during uncertain periods

This does not mean predicting the future perfectly, it means being more prepared and informed.

Making Smarter Financial Decisions

When you understand macroeconomics, you can make better decisions in your own life.

You can apply these ideas by:

- Paying attention to how inflation affects your spending
- Being aware of economic conditions when making large financial decisions
- Understanding how interest rates impact borrowing and saving

These small adjustments can make a meaningful difference over time.

Where to Go Next (If You Want to Learn More)

This book gives you the big picture, but there is always more to explore. If you want to go deeper, you can continue learning about:

- More detailed economic policy and strategy
- Investment and financial markets
- How global economies interact

The important part is that you now have a foundation to build on.

Last Thoughts

Macroeconomics is not something that only exists in textbooks or on the news. It is something that affects your everyday life, whether you notice it or not. Once you understand how growth, inflation, and policy decisions connect, you start to see the logic behind economic changes. As you move forward, remember this: the better you understand the big picture, the more confident you will be in navigating the world around you.

About the Author

Roggie "Raj" Clark is an entrepreneur and a 10-year marketing professional with a proven track record in e-commerce and digital business growth. Having built and managed successful online stores with thousands of sales and consulted for numerous marketing clients, Roggie has mastered the intricacies of online marketing, branding, and consumer behavior. He has also written several popular books on digital marketing, SEO (search engine optimization), and programming (HTML, CSS, and JavaScript).

As a former marketing manager at a fintech company—a role he secured through his own marketing and financial expertise—Roggie gained firsthand experience in financial strategy and wealth-building. This journey inspired him to share insights with amateur investors, helping them save money, make smarter financial decisions, and build long-term wealth. Raj currently lives in Maryland with his sister and niece.